# Wolf Coloring Book

## Realistic Adult Coloring Book, Advanced Wolf Coloring Book for Adults

### Realistic Animals Coloring Book: Vol 2

by Amanda Davenport

ISBN-13: 978-1530303632

ISBN-10: 153030363X

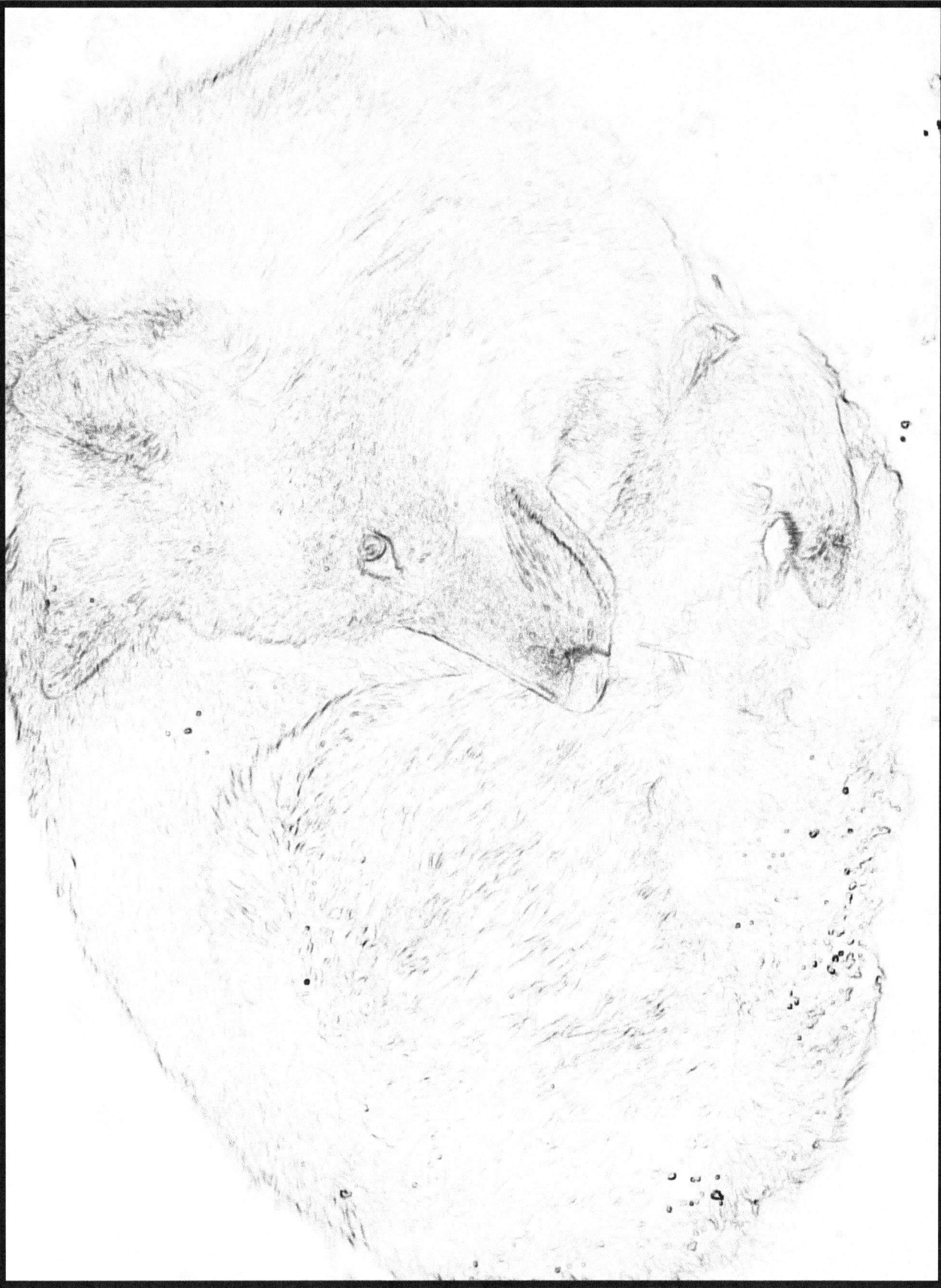

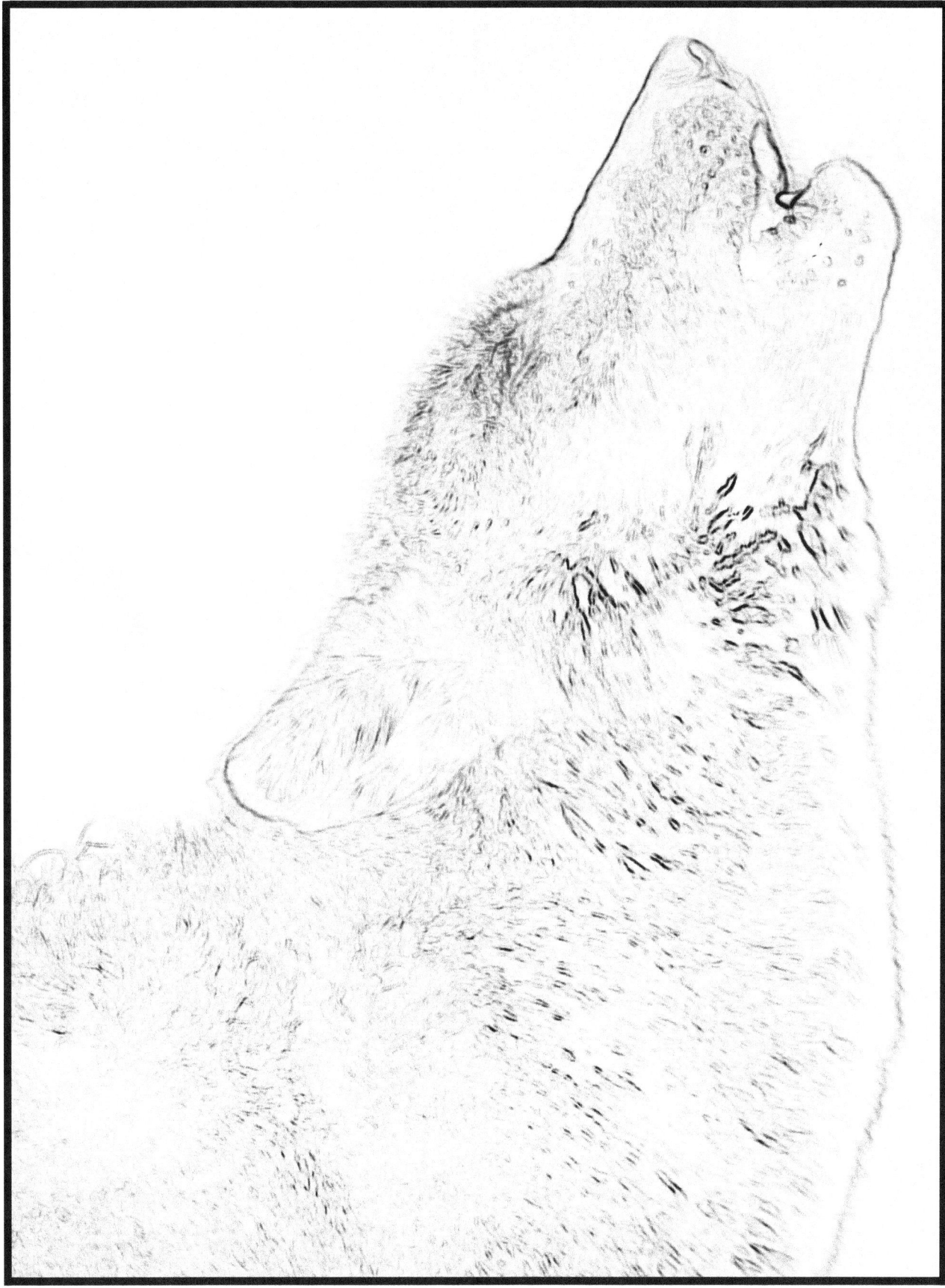

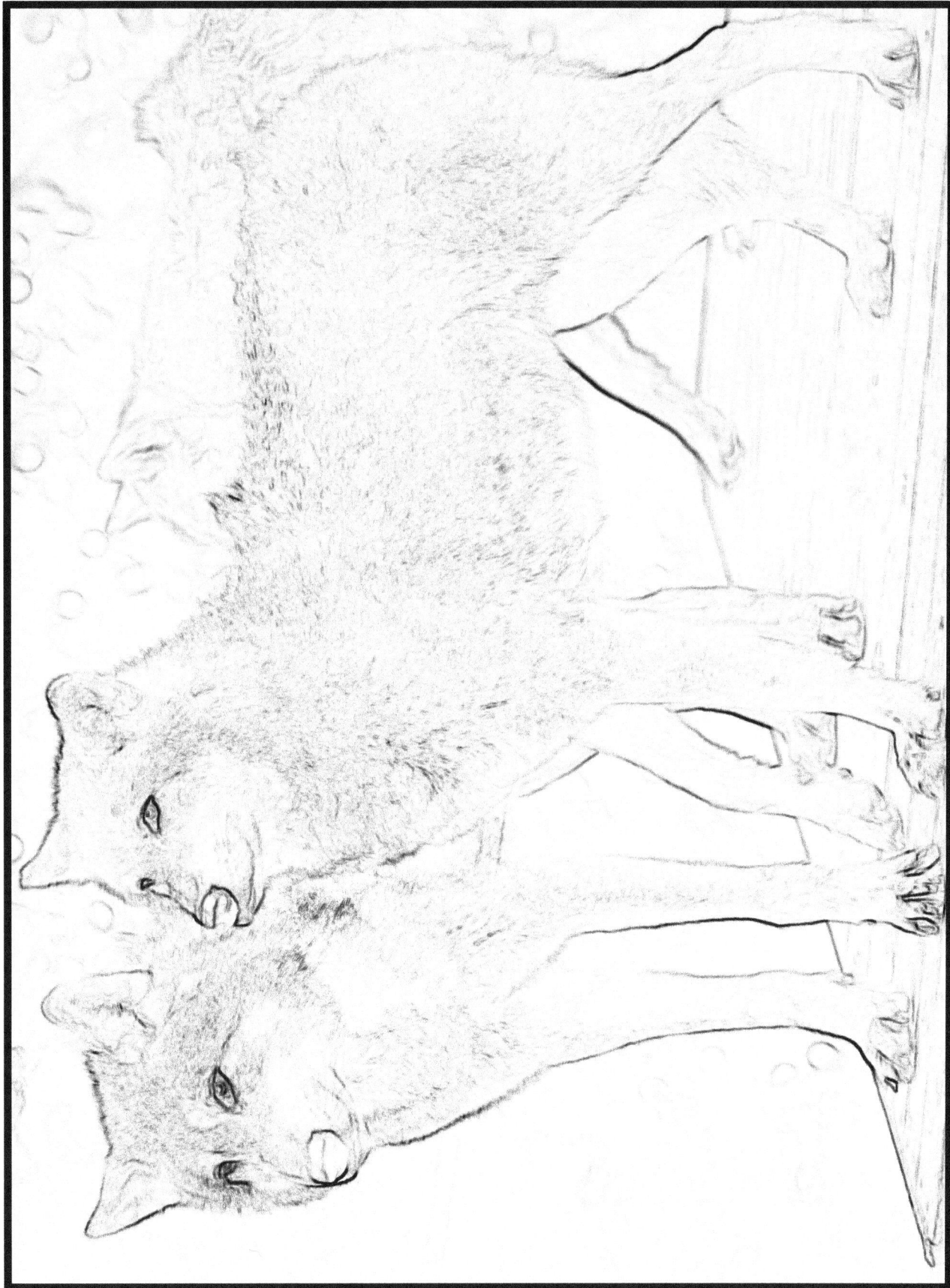

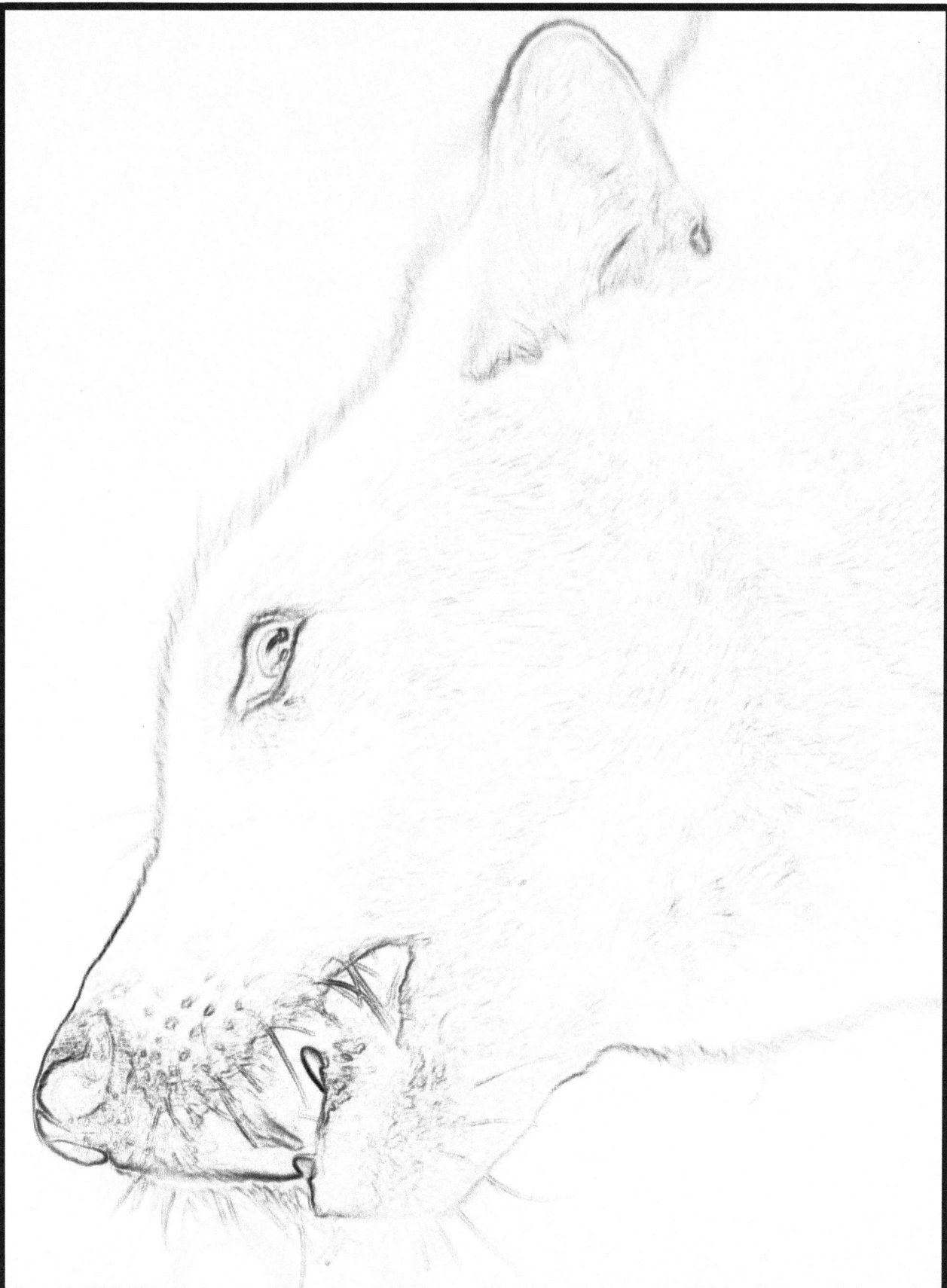

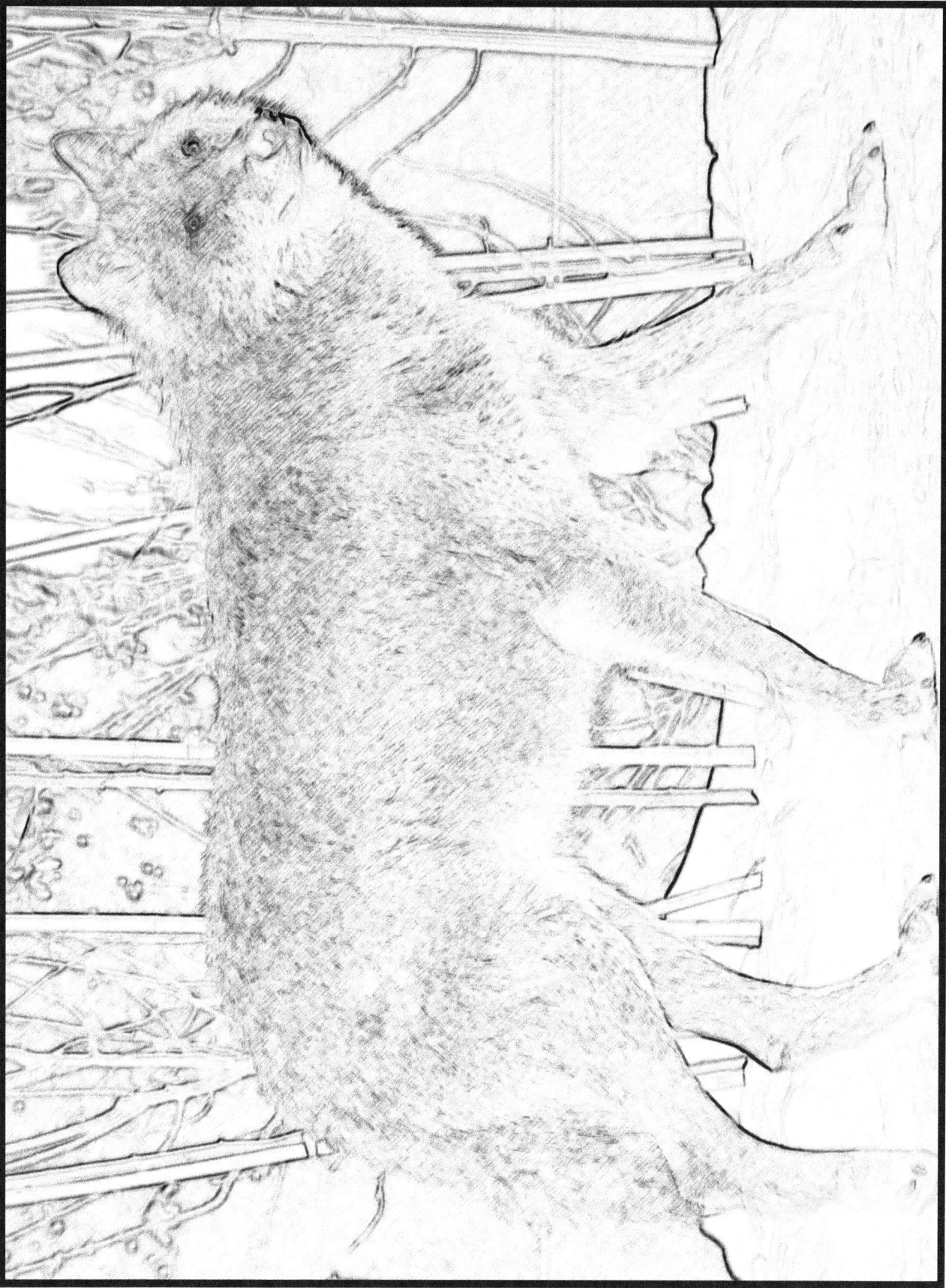

www.ingramcontent.com/pod-product-compliance
Lightning Source LLC
Chambersburg PA
CBHW081420280526
45788CB00009B/3168